The SAMURAI WARRIORS

Philip Steele

Illustrated by Nicki Palin

Kingfisher

NEW YORK

About this book

Samurai Warriors is almost like two books in one — a storybook to read and an information book to explore. Large, colorful illustrations and a simple narrative tell a story about the samurai, while the text under the folded pages provides a wealth of fascinating information.

If you are reading with a child, the unfolding of the flaps will give you the perfect opportunity to pause, answer questions, and discuss what is happening in the story. Children reading alone will enjoy discovering the extra details under the folds, especially as the information they find there will enhance their understanding of the story.

It is a sunny spring morning and Saburo and his sister Michiko are chasing butterflies by the shrine near their village. "Let's go and see if father has finished the sword," calls Michiko. "He says it is the best one he has ever made!"

3

The two children love to visit their father's workshop. There, he makes some of the finest samurai swords in all Japan. His workshop is a magical place, full of shadows and sparks, and ringing with the sound of hammers beating steel.

"Don't touch the blade, Saburo!" his father warns him. "It is very sharp. This sword is for the Lord of the White Castle himself."

However, the next day a troop of samurai thunders into the village. Their leader has heard about the sword and wants it for himself.

"But this sword is not mine to give," the swordsmith explains. "It belongs to the Lord of the White Castle."

"He won't need it," the angry general growls. "Give me the sword!"

The swordsmith has no choice. He bows, and hands it over.

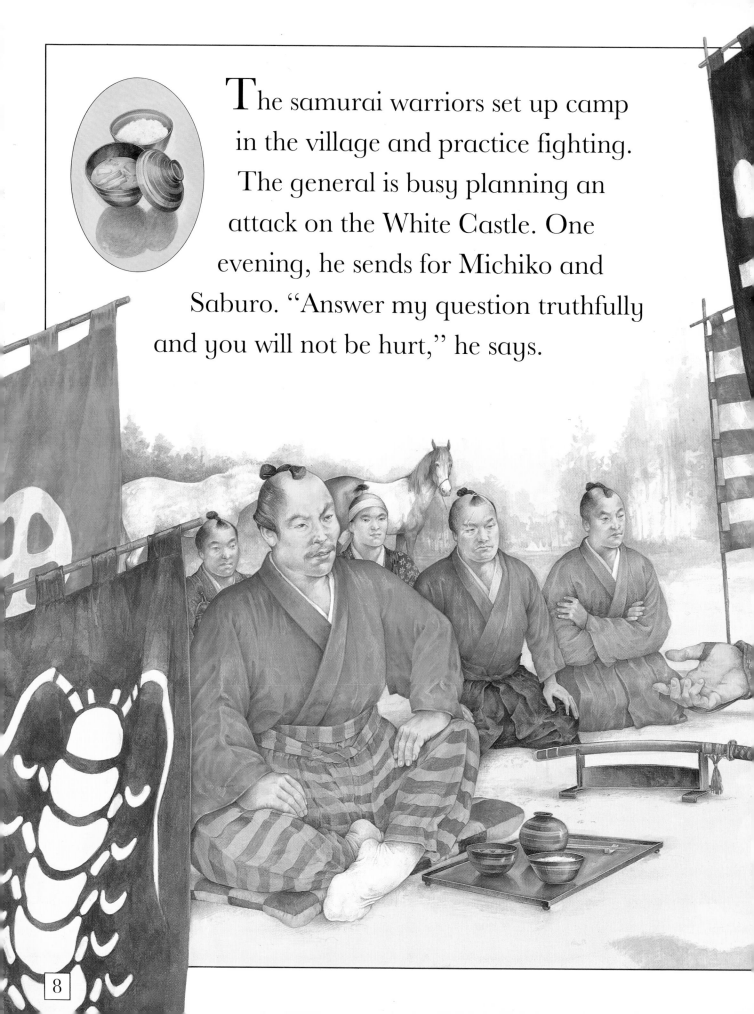

The samurai warriors set up camp in the village and practice fighting. The general is busy planning an attack on the White Castle. One evening, he sends for Michiko and Saburo. "Answer my question truthfully and you will not be hurt," he says.

"Do you know all the paths through the forest?" he asks. They nod, too scared to speak. "Excellent," he says with a cruel smile. "Tomorrow you will show us a secret way to the castle."

At dawn, the samurai get ready to leave. The White Castle is on the far side of the forest, half a day's march away. Two of the warriors lift Saburo and Michiko onto their horses.

"Which way?" snaps the general. The children point, and soon they are entering the gloomy forest. The paths are narrow and difficult to follow. By the time the army reaches the other side, the Sun is high in the sky.

The warriors stop to rest and put on their full armor ready for the battle. Michiko and Saburo watch from behind some trees. "What can we do?" Saburo whispers to his sister. "They are going to attack the castle and it's all our fault!"

"I have an idea," says Michiko. Quickly, she picks up a piece of shiny metal armor and flashes a warning signal to the castle guards.

On the castle walls, a sharp-eyed sentry spots the flashing light in the forest. He stares hard. He can just make out the shapes of horses and soldiers. "Sound the alarm!" he shouts to the drummer. The Lord of the Castle strides to a watchtower. He grips his sword when he sees the flags.

"It's the Lord of the Red River, my old enemy!"

The Lord of the Red River leads his army in a fierce charge toward the castle. But the defenders are ready for them! Deadly arrows rain down from the castle walls. Then the great gates swing open, and the Lord of the White Castle and his samurai gallop out. Sword clashes against sword in a furious battle.

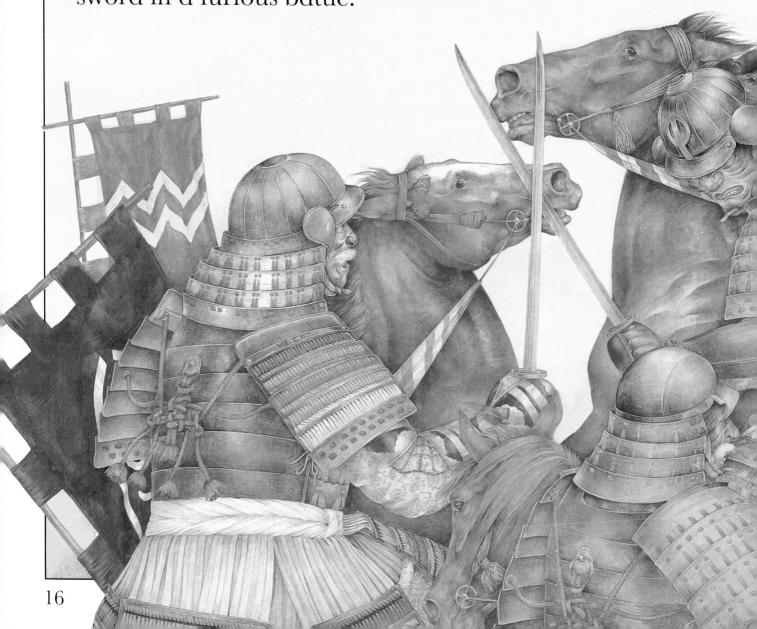

At last the fighting stops. "Can you see any enemy flags?" Saburo asks. "No!" laughs Michiko. They hug each other for joy. Together, they set off for the White Castle. As they cross the stream, Michiko notices something shining in the water.

"Look," she cries, "it's father's sword!" Just then, one of the castle guards gallops up. Michiko quickly tells him all that has happened.

"And this is the sword that our father made for the Lord of the Castle," she says. "Then you must present it to him yourselves," the samurai replies.

The Lord of the White Castle is so pleased with the children, he invites them to be his guests. That night, they listen to the music made by the *koto* player.

"Just look at those beautiful ladies," Michiko gasps.

"I wonder what they had for supper," whispers Saburo.

A servant overhears him and brings the hungry children all the fish and rice they can eat. Soon they fall asleep and are carried off to bed.

The next day, Michiko and Saburo can't wait to get home so they can tell their father all about their adventure. "I was proud of that fine samurai sword," he tells them. "But I am even prouder of my two brave children."

Index

When the page numbers are in **bold, like this,** it means you'll find the words under the folds.

KINGFISHER
Larousse Kingfisher Chambers Inc.
95 Madison Avenue
New York, New York 10016

First American edition 1994
2 4 6 8 10 9 7 5 3 1

LIBRARY OF CONGRESS CATALOGING-IN-PUBLICATION DATA
Steele, Philip.
The Samurai warriors / by Philip Steele. – 1st American ed.
p.   cm. – (Fold out, find out)
Includes index.
1. Samurai–Social life and customs–Juvenile literature.
[1. Samurai.   2. Japan–History.]   I. Title.   II. Series.
DS827.S3S74   1994
952–dc20   93-43401   CIP   AC

ISBN 1-85697-513-4
Printed in Singapore

Author: Philip Steele
Consultant: Stephen Turnbull
Series editor: Sue Nicholson
Editor: Brigid Avison
Design: Ben White Associates and Brian Robertson
Art editor: Christina Fraser
Main illustrations: Nicki Palin
Cartoons: Tony Kenyon (B.L.Kearley Ltd)

2.6 R.L. (SPACHE)